BLASTOFF!

EARTH AND THE MOON

BLASTOFF!

EARTH AND THE MOON

by Rebecca Stefoff

BENCHMARK BOOKS

MARSHALL CAVENDISH

NEW YORK

With special thanks to Roy A. Gallant, Southworth Planetarium, University of Southern Maine, for his careful review of the manuscript.

Benchmark Books
Marshall Cavendish Corporation
99 White Plains Road
Tarrytown, NY 10591-9001
www.marshallcavendish.com

Library of Congress Cataloging-in-Publication Data

Stefoff, Rebecca, date
Earth and the Moon / Rebecca Stefoff.
p. cm. — (Blastoff!)
Includes bibliographical references and index.
ISBN 0-7614-1235-2
1. Earth—Juvenile literature. 2. Moon—Juvenile literature. [1. Earth. 2. Moon.] I. Title. II. Series.
QB631.4 .S73 2001   550—dc21   00-054710

Printed in Italy
1 3 5 6 4 2

Photo Research by Anne Burns Images
Cover Photo: Photri

The photographs in this book are used by permission and through the courtesy of:
Photo Researchers: NASA, 7, 46, 55; Dr. Steve Gull/Dr. John Fielden/Dr. Alan Smith, 11; Michael Giannechini, 15; Bruce Herman, 16; John Sanford/Science Photo Library, 19, 22; John Chumack/Science Source, 27; Frank Zullo, 28; Joe Tucciarone/Science Photo Library, 47; Earth Satellite Corp/Science Photo Library, 51; Mark Garlick/Science Photo Library, 52; Julian Baum/Science Photo Library, 56. *Photri*: 8, 10, 13, 21, 24 (top and bottom), 31, 37, 44, 45, 49; Frank LaBua, 42. *Art Resource*: Scala, 32. *Sovfoto/Eastfoto*: 33. *NASA*: 35, 39, 41.

Book design by Clair Moritz-Magnesio

CONTENTS

1

PLANET OF WATER AND LIFE

Our home planet, Earth, is the third from the Sun. It differs from the other eight planets in the Solar System in several important ways. For one thing, it is the only one with large quantities of liquid water. For another, it is the only inhabited planet. It is also by far the best-known body in the Solar System. People have been exploring Earth for thousands of years. Although many questions remain, we have learned much about the forces that have molded our planet over billions of years. These same forces still shape the ever-changing world we live in today.

A ROCKY CORE

Earth feels solid, but the firm surface we live on is only a shell. Geologists, scientists who study Earth's materials and structure, have discovered that much of our planet is liquid.

Earth formed about 4.6 billion years ago when rocky masses orbiting the Sun slammed into each other and formed a globe. The energy of those impacts produced tremendous heat that melted the rocky matter, so that Earth's first surface was a molten sea. As it gradually cooled and hardened, the elements of which it was made separated. Most of the heavier ones sank inward to form the planet's core. Earth now consists of that central core with two main layers around it.

The core itself is in two layers, a ball within a ball. The solid inner core, making up almost 2 percent of Earth's total mass, is a dense

Earth, as seen from the Galileo spacecraft in December 1992. Cloud formations cover the Pacific Ocean, the largest body of water on the planet.

globe of heavy metals, chiefly iron and nickel. Temperatures in the inner core may reach 7,400 degrees Fahrenheit (4,100 Centigrade). Metals normally melt into liquid or vaporize into gas at such high temperatures, but the great weight of material pressing down from above keeps the inner core solid. Wrapped around the inner core is the outer core, a vast, deep sea of liquid metal that contains about 31 percent of the planetary mass. The outer core is cooler than the inner core but still extremely hot. It ends 1,800 miles (2,890 kilometers) below the Earth's surface.

Enclosing the core is a rock layer called the mantle. It contains 67 percent of Earth's mass and is made of some iron along with lighter elements such as magnesium and silicon. The mantle is solid, except for its upper part, the asthenosphere, which is partly melted and consists of basalt, a kind of rock.

The third and topmost major layer of Earth is its shell. Like the core and the mantle, the shell has two parts. The outer part is the

Earth is made up of many layers, but only its outer skin can be studied directly. The deepest holes ever dug have not gone through the planet's crust.

crust, the thin, hard surface that sits on the planet like the peel of an apple. The crust is made of rocks such as granite, shale, and marble. You can walk directly on the crust in some places, such as the peaks and slopes of many mountain ranges, but over much of Earth's surface it is covered by water or soil. The inner part of the shell, around 43 miles (70 kilometers) thick, is the lithosphere. It forms a buffer zone between the hot asthenosphere of the upper mantle and the cold outer crust.

A SHIFTING SURFACE

Movement and change are among Earth's defining qualities. Heat from deep within Earth causes the molten rock of the asthenosphere to rise slowly. This causes movement in the lithosphere, which floats on the asthenosphere. The lithosphere is like an immense jigsaw puzzle, consisting of six large pieces and about a dozen smaller ones fitting together.

Geologists call those pieces plates. Their upper surfaces are the continents and ocean bottoms that make up the outer crust of Earth. These plates—and the continents that they support—are not fixed in position. A process called plate tectonics moves them very slowly across Earth's surface, like giant rafts of solid rock sliding across a sea of rock.

The movement of the plates begins in the centers of the world's oceans, at formations on the seafloors called midocean ridges. Along a midocean ridge, hot material rises from the asthenosphere and softens the lithosphere. At the center of the ridge is an opening where magma, or molten basalt, wells up from the mantle, forcing the soft lithosphere seafloor apart on either side. The magma flows down the ridge, gradually cooling to become part of the seafloor. This outward pressure from the midocean ridges causes the seafloor to spread and widen, pushing the far edges of its plates against other plates. At some plate boundaries, one plate slides under the other in a process called subduction. The subducted portion of the plate gradually softens and slides down into the mantle. If one of the colliding plates is carrying a land mass, the collision may push up huge wrinkles of land, forming mountain ranges. The Himalayas, the world's highest mountains, are still being built as the northward-moving plate that supports India and Australia grinds slowly into the plate bearing Europe and Asia.

None of this happens quickly. The creeping continents travel only about 2 to 4 inches (5 to 10 centimeters) each year. Around 225 million years ago, Earth's land masses formed one giant supercontinent that scientists call Pangaea ("all earth"). The forces that caused subduction and the spreading of the seafloor slowly pulled Pangaea apart, and the continents drifted into their present positions. They will keep

The continents rode the shifting plates into their present positions. Earthquakes and volcanoes occur along the zones where plates meet.

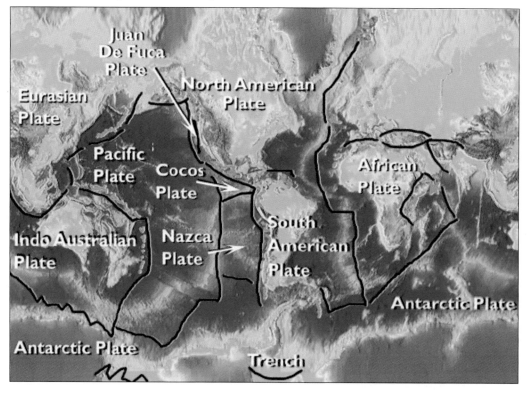

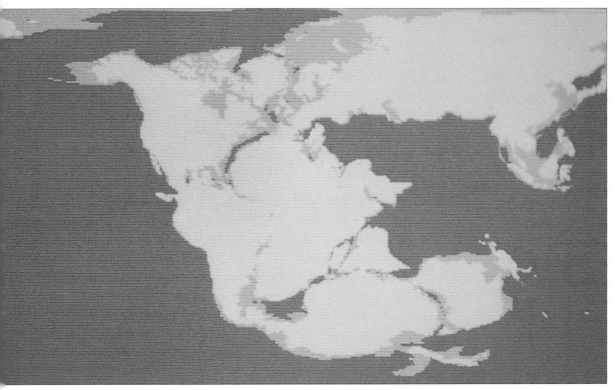

After Pangaea, the original supercontinent, began to break up, familiar land masses started to appear. This computer graphic shows Earth as it probably looked 200 million years ago.

drifting, and millions of years from now the outlines of Earth's continents and seas will be very different from those we know.

Plate boundaries can be turbulent places. Tremendous pressure builds up as plates scrape and grind against each other. Sometimes that force releases itself in sudden, violent plate movements we call earthquakes. Also along plate boundaries, magma from the melting, subducting lithosphere is pushed upward, occasionally oozing or shooting out onto Earth's surface through the vents known as volcanoes. So many volcanoes are active along the plate boundaries that border the Pacific Ocean that geologists call the ocean's rim the "Ring of Fire."

AIR, WATER, AND LIVING THINGS

Three spheres exist on and above Earth's surface. The atmosphere is the planet's air, the hydrosphere is its water, and the biosphere is the world of living things.

The atmosphere formed early in Earth's history, as the planet cooled and released gases from its interior. Kept from escaping into space by Earth's gravity, the gases formed an envelope or shell around the world. Originally that atmosphere consisted mostly of nitrogen and carbon dioxide. After plants appeared on Earth, they slowly changed the atmosphere over millions of years—plants draw carbon dioxide from the atmosphere and replace it with oxygen. The atmosphere now contains 78 percent nitrogen and 21 percent oxygen. The remaining 1 percent consists mostly of the gas argon, along with small amounts of water vapor, carbon dioxide, and other gases.

The atmosphere is made of various layers. The bottom layer, the troposphere, is between 5 and 12 miles (8 and 18 kilometers) thick. It contains the air we breathe and most of the planet's weather. Above the troposphere is the stratosphere. Reaching to about 30 miles (48 kilometers) above Earth's surface, the stratosphere contains a layer of gas called ozone that shields Earth from the Sun's burning ultraviolet rays. In the higher levels of the atmosphere, the air is extremely thin. A layer called the thermosphere extends 400 miles (650 kilometers) above Earth's surface. Beyond that the atmosphere ends, and outer space begins.

The original atmosphere held a certain amount of water vapor. As the atmosphere cooled, the water vapor turned from a gas into a liquid and fell as rain, collecting to form oceans, lakes, and rivers. About 71 percent of Earth's surface is covered with water. Most of this water is in the oceans, which contain minerals dissolved from rock. Sea water tastes salty because one of its most abundant minerals is sodium chloride, which we use to salt our food. Only about 2 percent

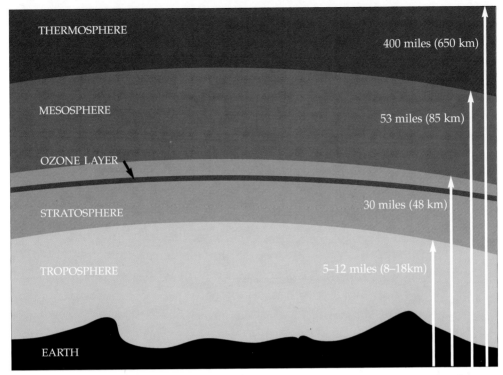

THERMOSPHERE

400 miles (650 km)

MESOSPHERE

53 miles (85 km)

OZONE LAYER

STRATOSPHERE

30 miles (48 km)

TROPOSPHERE

5–12 miles (8–18km)

EARTH

One part of the atmosphere, the ozone layer, protects Earth from the ultraviolet light of the Sun's rays. Human activities, such as putting certain chemicals into the atmosphere, are gradually erasing that layer. One likely effect of ozone loss is an increased rate of skin cancer.

of the planet's water is fresh, with little or no salt. Sunlight evaporates water from the oceans and turns it into water vapor. If the water vapor cools, it becomes liquid again and falls as rain. Some fresh water is in lakes, ponds, and rivers, and some is in natural underground reservoirs called aquifers. But 80 percent of all the fresh water on Earth is frozen, either at the north and south poles, on Greenland, or high in the mountains.

Earth's biosphere may be unique. As far as we know, no other world in the Solar System or anywhere else supports life, although some scientists think that life has probably appeared many times in the universe. Astronomers are now examining rocks from Mars in an effort to see whether they might hold fossilized traces of tiny living things.

Earth's Invisible Umbrella

Earth produces a magnetic field that scientists think is probably created by electrical currents moving through the planet's liquid outer core. The magnetic force is strongest in a region called the magnetosphere, which begins about 90 miles (140 kilometers) above Earth's surface. The magnetosphere surrounds the planet and traps electrical particles, such as electrons and protons, as they travel through space from the Sun. If the magnetosphere did not exist, those particles would strike the unprotected Earth in a shower of electricity that would be fatal to life as we know it.

The protective magnetosphere is invisible to human eyes. Sometimes, however, it creates eerily beautiful light shows called auroras that people living far north or south of the equator can see. The magnetosphere captures electrically charged particles and pulls them toward the North and South Poles, where they collide with atoms in the atmosphere, producing rippling, glowing sheets and ribbons of light in the night sky.

Collisions between particles in the upper atmosphere create what environmentalist John Muir called "this glory of light, so pure, so bright, so enthusiastic in motion."

Life appeared in the seas of Earth about 3.5 billion years ago. Scientists are not sure how it originated, but most believe that electrical discharges from lightning interacted with chemical compounds in the oceans to produce cells of living matter. For ages, the only living things on the planet were one-celled ocean plants called algae. Then, hundreds of millions or perhaps even several billion years ago, more complex organisms, consisting of groups of cells joined together, evolved in the oceans. Life next appeared on land—plants first, followed by animals.

Algae on an Alaskan mudflat. Early in Earth's history, these plants were not just the highest form on life of the planet, they were the only form.

Naming the World

Our planet has had almost as many names as there are languages. Today, most English-speaking people call it Earth. The ancient Greeks called it Gaea or Gaia, a name from Greek and Roman mythology, the source of all the other planets' names. The mythological Gaea was the earth in the form of a great goddess, the mother and wife of Uranus, the sky. Another name for our planet is Terra, the Latin word for earth or ground. From Terra comes terrestrial, which means "having to do with Earth."

Life has evolved into a great variety of types, or species. Palm trees and dandelions, massive dinosaurs that stomped across the land and the tiny parasites that lurked in their bloodstreams, bats and butterflies, horses and seahorses, human beings and bacteria—the diversity of life is beyond the imagination of even the most inventive science-fiction writer. Scientists do not know how many species exist today, because new ones are still being discovered. Their estimates range from 1.5 million species to as many as 10 million or more. Still, these are just a fraction of the total number of species that have inhabited Earth. More than 99 percent of all species that have ever lived are now extinct. They have vanished except for a few bones and footprints, preserved as fossils by time and chance.

2

Dance of Two Worlds

arth has a partner in its dance around the Sun. Along with Earth travels its single natural satellite, the Moon. About one-quarter the size of Earth, the Moon is the fifth largest of the dozens of known moons in the Solar System. Earth and the Moon are held together by gravitation, the same force that links the planets to the Sun. The relationships among these three bodies produce effects as ordinary as sunrise and nightfall and as strange as the temporary disappearance of the Sun or Moon in the form of an eclipse.

DAYS, YEARS, AND SEASONS

No one ever really stands still. Human senses do not perceive the Earth's motion, but our planet is continuously moving, whirling around like a top (rotating) at the same time it is racing around the Sun (revolving).

Picture a pole running through the center of the world from north to south, like a skewer through a marshmallow. That line is Earth's axis. The world rotates, or spins, around the axis. One rotation equals a complete cycle of day and night. The Sun does not rise and set over a motionless Earth—words such as *sunrise* and *sunset* simply describe how the Sun's motions appear from Earth. Earth's rotation exposes each part of the planet to day (when that part faces the Sun) and night (when it is turned away from the Sun).

The day, defined by Earth's rotation, is a basic unit of time meas-

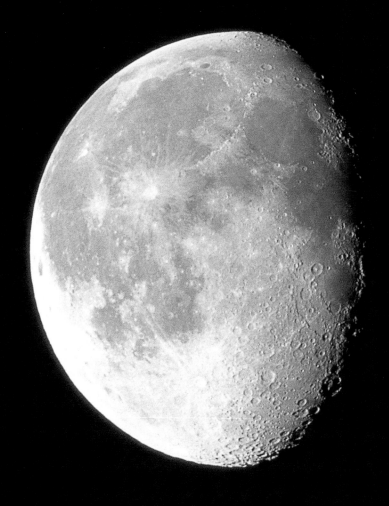

A waning gibbous Moon, the name of one of its phases. Some early calendars were based on the lunar cycle, the source of our unit of time, the month.

urement. Another unit, the year, is defined by Earth's revolution around the Sun. Traveling at 18.5 miles per second (29.8 km/sec), Earth completes an orbit around the Sun every 365.25 days. This revolution gives us the 365-day year, with an extra quarter of a day left over each year. Different cultures have come up with various ways of keeping those quarter days from piling up. Today the most common method is to add an extra day to the calendar every fourth year.

Earth's orbit around the Sun is level, as if the planet were rolling

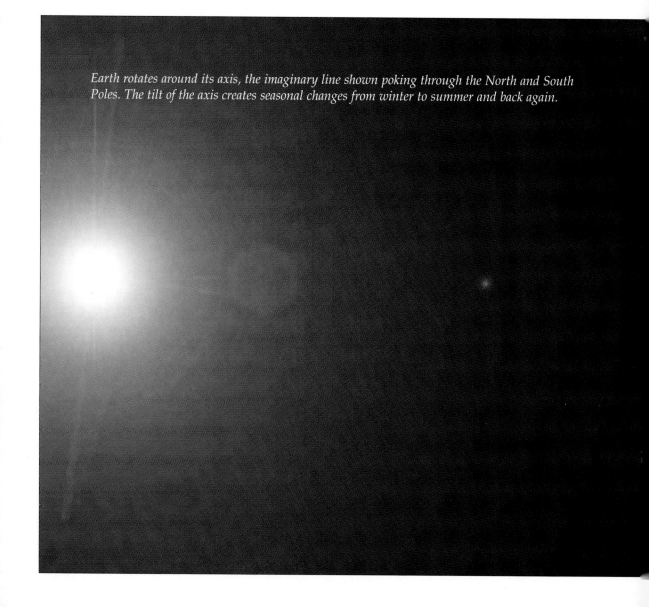

Earth rotates around its axis, the imaginary line shown poking through the North and South Poles. The tilt of the axis creates seasonal changes from winter to summer and back again.

on the edge of a plate with the Sun in the middle. That imaginary plate is called the plane of Earth's orbit. If Earth's axis extended straight up and down from the plane of orbit, Earth's season would never change. But the axis is tilted at an angle of 23.5 degrees to the plane of orbit. This means that during part of Earth's annual revolution, the North Pole is tipped toward the Sun and the South Pole is tipped away. At the opposite side of the orbit, the South Pole is tipped toward the Sun and the North Pole is tipped away. Summer occurs in

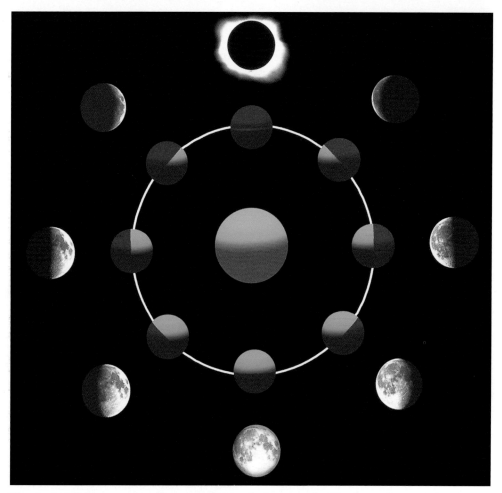

The photos of the outer ring show the phases of a lunar cycle. The inner diagram shows how sunlight reaches Earth (center) and the Moon at each phase.

each hemisphere when that hemisphere is tipped toward the Sun. When the hemisphere tips away from the Sun, winter follows.

THE PHASES OF THE MOON

Days, years, and seasons are all defined by the relationship between Earth and the Sun. Another unit of time measurement, the month, is defined by the Moon's revolution around Earth. Like the Sun, the Moon appears to rise in the east and set in the west, but unlike the Sun it changes shape from night to night, and for part of each month it seems to be completely absent. These changes have to do with the source of moonlight. The Sun gives off light, but the silvery beams that we call moonlight do not come from the Moon, which makes no light of its own. Moonlight is really sunlight reflected from the Moon's surface. As the Moon revolves around Earth, the Sun shines on different portions of the lunar surface, causing the Moon to pass through a cycle called the lunar phases.

When the Moon is between the Sun and the Earth, no sunlight reaches the side of the Moon facing the Earth, which remains dark. We call this phase the new moon or the dark of the moon. A day or two later, when the Moon is a little farther along in its orbit, sunlight strikes its curved right rim—the crescent moon phase. Night after night more of the Moon appears. When the entire right half of its surface shows, we say that it has reached the first quarter phase because it has completed one-fourth of its cycle. About a week later comes the full moon, when the Moon is completely illuminated. In another week the Moon reaches the last quarter phase, when only its left half appears. After a crescent phase that highlights its left rim, the Moon grows dark again, and the cycle of phases starts anew.

The cycle of phases, called the synodic month, takes 29.5 days. Ancient peoples started every month at the new moon, and every month was 29.5 days long. Some cultures, including Muslim ones, still use this lunar calendar. The United States, Europe, and many other parts of the world have added extra days to most months to make 12 months equal to 365 days, or one year.

Although the Moon's phases keep changing, it has the same face turned to Earth at all times. One hemisphere of the Moon, the near side, is always visible from Earth. The other, the far side, is always turned away from Earth.

*The Moon's handiwork—
high tide . . .
. . . and low tide at a coastal
community in France.*

TIDES

The Moon causes the tides, an important feature of Earth's hydrosphere. These regular risings and fallings of ocean levels, called high and low tides, occur when the Moon's gravity affects the oceans. Each part of the world has two high tides a day, once when the Moon is overhead and once when it is exactly on the other side of the world. Midway between the two high tides are the two low tides. Tidal risings and fallings vary from place to place because of differences in the depth of the water, the ocean currents, and the shape of the sea bottom. In some places, the tides are barely noticeable, while in a few locations, such as Canada's Bay of Fundy, they may surge and drop as much as 50 feet (15 meters).

The Sun's gravitational pull is stronger than the Moon's, but the Sun is much farther away, so its tidal force on Earth is less than a third of the Moon's. When the Sun and Moon are in a straight line with Earth, the Sun adds its gravitational pull to the Moon's to create the strongest tidal forces. These produce the highest and lowest tides, called spring tides, although they can occur at any time of year.

ECLIPSES

The Roman historian Livy described an event that disturbed the people of ancient Rome on July 17, 188 B.C. He wrote that "in the daytime at the third hour darkness has covered everything." The authorities ordered a special three-day period of prayer at all street-corner shrines because of this unnatural darkness, thought to be a sign of coming trouble.

The strange darkness that upset the Romans was a solar eclipse, during which part or all of the Sun seems to disappear. The same thing happens to the Moon during a lunar eclipse. Ancient and medieval records from around the world contain references to more

WHAT IF THE MOON DIDN'T EXIST?

In a 1993 book titled *What If the Moon Didn't Exist? Voyages to Earths that Might Have Been*, astronomer Neil F. Comins wondered what our planet would be like under different conditions. In describing a moonless Earth, he showed how the Moon has shaped the course of life on Earth.

You might think that Earth would be pretty much the same without the Moon, but Comins points out that without the Moon, tides would be lower. Days would also be shorter, because the Moon's gravitational force has gradually slowed the Earth's rotation over time, leading to longer and longer days. Without the Moon, Earth would rotate faster. Winds and waves would be much higher, making Earth's weather much more ferocious. High winds might prevent tall trees from evolving, and that might mean that tree-dwelling creatures such as our distant ancestors would not exist. Life on a moonless Earth would almost certainly take far different forms than the life we know. And if intelligent life did arise on that moonless Earth, Comins suggests that it might never develop spaceflight without a bright, beckoning world right on its doorstep to serve as its first goal.

What would be one of the most obvious results of moonlessness? Dark nights. The Moon is such a familiar sight that most people could not think of nighttime without it.

Multiple exposures on a single photograph trace the stages of a solar eclipse as the Sun rises over Texas. In the top image, the shadow of the Moon has begun to pull away. Light will soon return to an unnaturally dark day.

than a thousand eclipses of the Sun or the Moon. People often thought they were warnings of disasters, such as the deaths of kings. Today, astronomers know when solar and lunar eclipses will occur and from where on Earth they will be visible. They also understand the causes of eclipses, which have nothing to do with human affairs.

Eclipses occur when the Sun, Moon, and Earth line up in certain ways. When Earth is between the Sun and the Moon, Earth casts a shadow that can fall across the Moon. When this happens, the shadow appears to creep across the surface of the Moon as the Moon travels through the shadowed area of space. For more than an hour the Moon is completely eclipsed, then the shadow slowly withdraws in the other direction. During totality, the period when the entire lunar surface is eclipsed, the shadowed Moon may glow with a dim, reddish light—perfect for those ancient skywatchers who saw eclipses as omens of war and bloodshed.

When the Moon is between Earth and the Sun, a solar eclipse may occur. The Moon casts a shadow that falls on Earth, although the shadow is small and covers only part of Earth's surface. People inside that shadowed area see the Moon pass in front of the Sun, slowly darkening all or part of its surface. Sunlight becomes faint and eerie, and stars appear in the daytime sky. The period of totality in a solar eclipse never lasts longer than about seven minutes—not long, but enough to frighten people who did not know what made the Sun "go out." Total eclipses are rare. In any given part of Earth, they occur once about every 350 years. No wonder people once thought of them as history-making events.

3

DESTINATION MOON

The Moon is the first world—and so far the only world—that humans have visited. On July 20, 1969, astronauts stepped onto the lunar surface for the first time. For thousands of years before that day, people had been fascianted by the Moon, our closest neighbor in space.

FROM MYTH TO SCIENCE

To many ancient cultures, the Moon seemed to be a goddess, perhaps the wife or sister of the Sun god. Looking at the pattern of dark and bright patches on the Moon, people imagined that the markings formed patterns, such as the face of the "Man in the Moon."

The ancient Greeks reached a more scientific understanding of the Moon. They knew that it is a spherical body in space, orbiting the Earth, and that its light is reflected sunlight. They even understood that a lunar eclipse is Earth's shadow cast on the Moon, and from observations of that shadow during eclipses they knew that Earth is round. Some Greek and Roman thinkers suggested that the Moon was similar to Earth, with people living on it. They thought that its dark patches were oceans and that its light patches were land. This is why the Moon's dark areas are still called *maria*, which means "seas" in Latin, the ancient Roman language.

The first person to study the Moon through a telescope was the Italian scientist Galileo Galilei. He drew detailed sketch maps of the

Unless a meteorite strikes them or a passerby tramples them, the footprints of the Apollo astronauts will remain pressed into the windless, rainless lunar surface forever.

Moon's surface, showing a world covered with mountains and craters. He published them in 1610. Later in the 1600s, astronomers began producing more detailed Moon maps, and they developed a system of naming lunar features that is still used. The craters are named after scientists and philosophers. Names of the *maria* refer to the weather, such as the Sea of Clouds, or to states of mind, such as the Sea of Tranquillity.

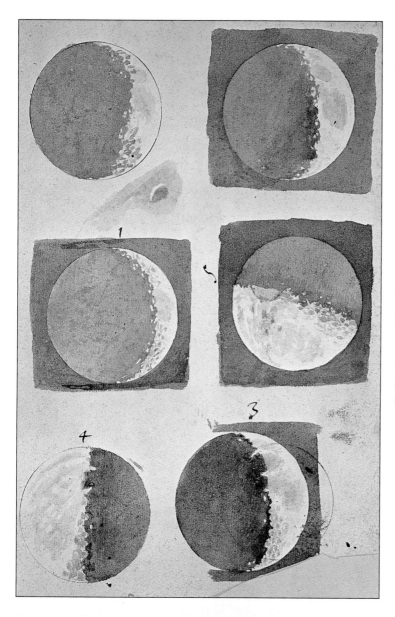

Galileo's drawings of the Moon, the first to be made with the help of a telescope, startled people in the 1600s. Most had expected the Moon to be smooth and unmarked because it appeared to be so in the sky.

Sputnik 1, *the first artificial satellite, began the space race that carried American astronauts to the Moon.*

THE SPACE RACE

World War II (1939–1945) brought great advances in rocket science, and after the war some nations continued to investigate its possibilities. Their research had a military basis. At the time, the United States was locked in a hostile rivalry with the Soviet Union, which at the time included Russia and a number of neighboring states. These two superpowers competed to master the skies, each fearing that the other might use rockets or spacecraft for spying or dropping bombs. This competition became known as the "space race," and it spurred the two nations to develop new technology and eventually to travel beyond Earth's atmosphere.

A milestone in the space race occurred in 1957, when the Soviet Union launched a rocket that carried the first artifical satellite, *Sputnik*, into orbit around Earth. Two years later, the Soviets sent three unmanned space probes to the Moon. *Luna 1* flew past the Moon, *Luna 2* became the first humanmade object ever to reach the Moon's surface, and *Luna 3* traveled around the Moon, taking the first pictures of its far side. These achievements alarmed the Americans, who became even more disturbed in 1961, when Yuri Gagarin of the Soviet

Moon Crazy

Luna was an ancient Roman name for the Moon goddess and for the Moon itself. It gave rise to the word *lunatic*, meaning an insane person, because people once thought that the Moon's rays could drive one insane. Even today you may hear someone say that the full Moon brings an increase in crime, admissions to hospitals, or just plain crazy behavior. This is a myth. As reported in the journal *Skeptical Inquirer*, several well-run studies since the 1980s have shown that the phases of the Moon have no effect on physical or mental illness or on the rate of criminal activity.

Union became the first human being to travel in space. Determined not to be beaten by the Soviets, the United States poured funds into a space program of its own, establishing the National Aeronautics and Space Administration (NASA) to oversee it.

Beginning in 1962, NASA sent several series of probes to the Moon. Soviet *Luna* probes were the first to orbit the Moon and to make soft landings (controlled landings, not crashes) on the lunar surface. But American *Ranger*, *Surveyor*, and *Lunar Orbiter* probes were not far behind. These spacecraft gathered new and valuable information about the Moon and broadcast it back to scientists on Earth. Photographs taken by cameras aboard the probes led to the most accurate maps of the Moon to date. The probes were even able to analyze the lunar surface, proving that the *maria* were covered with volcanic material, as some scientists had suspected. These were major achievements, but the political leaders who directed NASA felt that the most important part of the space race was sending humans to the Moon—and bringing them back again, of course.

THE APOLLO PROGRAM

By 1969 NASA had sent a number of successful probes to the Moon. NASA had also operated its Gemini program, which trained astronauts to guide and maneuver spacecraft, and its Apollo program, which developed a spacecraft that could reach the Moon. Three astronauts aboard *Apollo 8* had orbited the Moon in December 1968. They were the first people to get a close look at the Moon's near side and the first ever to see its far side. NASA decided that the time had come to seize the lead in space travel from the Soviets with a manned landing on the Moon.

With Earth hanging in the background, astronauts taking part in the Apollo 9 *mission practice a spacewalk.*

WHO OWNS THE MOON?

No one owns the Moon—or everyone does. You can buy a piece of real estate on the Moon from an Internet site, but be warned: Beyond its entertainment value, your "claim" to lunar land is worthless.

A few people have claimed to own the Moon, according to the Institute of Air and Space Law at Leiden University in the Netherlands. One is an American businessman who offers to sell lunar real estate and has tried to claim the Moon under the 1862 U.S. Homestead Act. Another is a German citizen whose distant ancestor received a "gift" of the Moon from his king. Neither claim has legal merit. In 1959 the United Nations established the Committee for the Peaceful Uses of Outer Space (COPSUO) to develop international laws for space. One law, the Outer Space Treaty, went into effect in 1967. It says that no nation can lay claim to the Moon, but it did not outlaw the use of lunar resources. COPSUO wrote a more strongly worded document called the Moon Treaty, which would prevent public or private ownership of lunar land, ban weapons on the Moon, and create a special space government to distribute the profits from any mining or other activities on the Moon to all nations. Few countries have signed this treaty, and the United States—the only nation that has so far sent people to the Moon—is not expected to do so. Some think that the uninhabited frontier of the Moon and planets may one day be settled or used by whatever nation, corporation, research institute, or private investor gets to them first.

Feel like homesteading on the Moon? You can buy a parcel of this undeveloped real estate, but your claim has no legal status—and getting to your property won't be easy.

In March 1969 NASA launched *Apollo 9*, which orbited Earth. Its astronauts tested a smaller spacecraft called the Lunar Module (LM), designed to be sent down to the Moon's surface during a lunar mission. Two months later the *Apollo 10* crew orbited the Moon. The LM separated from the main part of the spacecraft, called the command/service module or CSM, and orbited the Moon safely on its own before docking with the CSM to return to Earth.

NASA was now ready for its next historic step. *Apollo 11* lifted off from Florida on July 16, 1969, atop a 3,200-ton (3,251-metric tons) *Saturn V* rocket. The spacecraft separated from the rocket booster and headed toward the Moon. Four days later the LM, named *Eagle*, separated from the CSM. Carrying astronauts Neil Armstrong and Edwin "Buzz" Aldrin, it descended toward the Moon's surface. Armstrong saw that it was headed for a boulder-strewn area inside a crater and made some last-minute adjustments to land the *Eagle* on a flat plain. He radioed to mission control in Houston, Texas: "The *Eagle* has landed." When Armstrong left the LM, he became the first human being to set foot on another world.

Armstrong and Aldin spent more than two hours on the Moon's surface, collecting rocks for scientific study and planting a U.S. flag. Their successful mission and safe return encouraged NASA to send more missions to the Moon over the next few years. The *Apollo 12* astronauts set up scientific equipment in the Ocean of Storms. *Apollo 13* never reached the Moon—an explosion on the spacecraft forced the astronauts to return to Earth, which they were lucky to reach. *Apollo 14*'s astronauts walked in the lunar highlands. The astronauts of the next three missions covered still more territory using a motorized rover that could reach speeds of 10 miles (16 kilometers) per hour. While the astronauts from the LMs performed experiments, set up equipment to radio information back to Earth, and collected geological samples, those who remained in the orbiting CSMs operated cameras and sensors that gathered valuable information about the Moon's surface features, magnetism, and gravity.

Apollo 17 in December 1972 was the first mission to include a trained geologist. This mission spent a record twenty-five hours exploring the rim of the Sea of Serenity and collected more geological samples than any of the earlier missions. But the *Apollo 17* astronauts knew that theirs was the last Apollo mission. The U.S. government and NASA had already decided that the Apollo program had realized its goals. The next stage in lunar exploration would take place on Earth, where scientists would spend many years studying the information and samples gathered by the Apollo missions.

The last Apollo mission landed in a rugged area between the Sea of Serenity and the Sea of Tranquillity, labeled here in their Latin names.

4

Our Spectacular Satellite

Information gathered by probes and astronauts has greatly increased our knowledge of the Moon. New facts have helped scientists form new ideas about our satellite's history, structure, and relationship with Earth. Together with the astronauts' descriptions of what it was like to walk on the Moon, this wealth of information paints a picture of conditions on our satellite—a world where unprotected humans would die instantly.

THE LUNAR ENVIRONMENT

The Moon has about one-sixth the gravitational pull of Earth, which means that an astronaut who weighed 200 pounds (90 kilograms) on Earth would weigh just 32 pounds (14 kilograms) on the Moon. The space suits and oxygen packs that the *Apollo* astronauts had to wear on the Moon weighed just about that much by themselves!

The low gravity means that you could jump six times as high or as far on the Moon as on Earth. It also explains why the Moon has almost no atmosphere. Billions of years ago, elements in the form of gas escaped from the Moon's interior to its surface, just as they did on Earth. The Moon's gravity was too weak to hold the gases, which escaped into space. The Moon still emits small amounts of gases, giving the Moon a very thin atmosphere that consists mostly of neon, hydrogen, helium, and argon. This atmosphere is so minimal that for practical purposes the Moon is an airless world. It is also a silent

Dwarfed by a massive rock, this lunar rover let the Apollo 17
astronauts cover more territory and gather more rock
samples than any previous crew.

world, without enough atmosphere to carry sound waves.

Because a complete lunar day is one Earth month long, the daytime and nighttime halves of the lunar day each lasts about two weeks at any point on the Moon's surface. During the daytime, the surface exposed to the Sun can reach temperatures as high as 214 degrees Fahrenheit (101 degrees C). Temperatures during the long lunar night can plunge to -300 degrees F (-184 degrees C). The Moon has no weather and no seasons—its axis is not tilted to the plane of its orbit as Earth's is. Day and night are always the same length and fea-

Many artists have used science and imagination to create moonscapes. This image, with Earth hanging in the lunar sky, mistakenly features clouds on the lunar horizon—impossible on an airless satellite.

ture the same temperatures on most of the Moon's surface. But a few small areas near the poles may be locked into eternal "winter." Scientists believe that parts of some deep craters may be permanently shadowed by the surrounding walls of rock.

THE MOONSCAPE

The lunar landscape has two main types of terrain, visible from Earth as dark and light patches. The dark patches are flat plains, the *maria* that were once thought to be seas. The bright ones are mountainous areas called lunar highlands.

All of the *maria* together cover 16 percent of the Moon's surface. Most of them are on the side of the Moon that faces Earth—scientists do not yet know why. They do know that the *maria* are covered with basalt. Billions of years ago it flowed up as molten magma, or lava, from 100 miles (160 kilometers) beneath the Moon's surface. The *maria* occur inside vast, saucer-shaped formations called impact basins, created when large meteorites struck the Moon early in its history. In some cases, these impacts created cracks and fractures through which magma from the Moon's interior could reach the surface and spread out in wide floods, forming the maria. Not all impact basins, however, are filled with *maria*. The largest impact basin, located near the south pole on the Moon's far side, is the Aitken Basin, about 1,550 miles (2,500 kilometers) wide.

The lunar highlands cover 84 percent of the Moon's surface and include mountain ranges as well as areas of hills, ridges, and broken terrain. Some of the mountains are the edges of impact basins, driven skyward as the impact flattened and spread the centers of the basins. For example, part of the rim of the 1,118-mile (1,800-kilometer) Imbrium Basin on the Moon's near side forms the Apennine Mountains, the tallest range on the Moon with peaks more than 20,000 feet (6,000 meters) high.

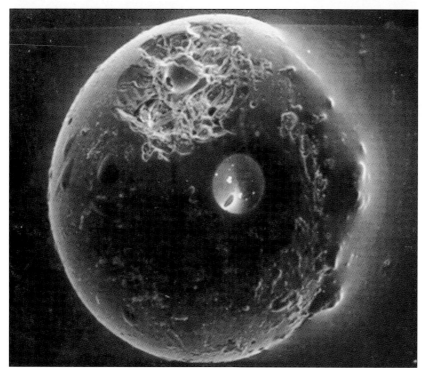

An image of the Moon? No, this tiny glass bead, called a spherule, is one of many found in soil samples from the Moon. Impacts cause lunar rock to melt and splash. When the rock cools, it sometimes forms spherules. This microscopic spherule bears a crater left by the impact of an even tinier micrometeorite.

Most of the lunar surface is covered with craters. Scientists think that the most important force in shaping the lunar surface has been bombardment by objects as large as asteroids and as small as grains of dust. The largest objects caused the huge impact basins when they struck the Moon. Smaller meteorites created thousands upon thousands of craters, flat or bowl-shaped depressions with raised edges. Craters of all sizes, from many miles or kilometers to just a few inches or centimeters across, cover the Moon's surface. However, fewer of them are visible in the *maria* than in the highlands because molten basalt has flowed over the surfaces of the *maria* in the past, covering many craters. Some of the larger craters have central peaks made of material forced up from deep within the Moon by the impacts that caused these craters. Some of the smaller craters were created when material thrown out from a large impact struck the lunar surface, causing a cluster of secondary impacts in the area. A few large craters, such as Tycho, Copernicus, and Kepler, can be seen from Earth because they are surrounded by patterns of bright streaks that extend for great distances across the Moon's surface. These streaks glow brilliantly, especially during the full moon. They consists of light-colored or glassy material splashed across the surface by the impacts that formed the craters.

Impacts by large objects are infrequent. But tiny micrometeorites the size of grains of sand rain down upon the Moon steadily (they rain down upon Earth, too, but burn up in its atmosphere). Over billions of years the micrometeorites have pounded the rocks of the lunar surface into a layer of fine, powdery dust called the regolith. In the *maria*, the regolith is 6.6 feet (2 meters) to 26 feet (8 meters) thick. It may be several times thicker in parts of the highlands. One of NASA's major concerns about the *Apollo* landings was whether astronauts could walk on the regolith without sinking into it. The first probes to land on the Moon, however, showed that objects (and people) sink only a few inches or centimeters into the regolith.

Copernicus, one of the Moon's largest craters, was named for the Polish astronomer who revolutionized astronomy by proving that the Sun, not the Earth, is the center of the Solar System and that the planets revolve around it.

A 50-mile-wide (80-kilometer) lunar crater photographed from the Apollo 11 spacecraft. Scientists know this is an old crater because later impacts have created many smaller craters within it and on its rim.

GEOLOGIC HISTORY AND INNER STRUCTURE

The Moon's surface was initially molten. As on Earth, heavier elements sank and lighter ones rose to the surface, which had cooled and solidified by about 4.3 billion years ago. For millions of years after that time, the lunar surface was bombarded as the Moon swept up most of the remaining debris in its orbit, creating the impact basins and many of the craters. Heat and energy from some of these impacts melted the subsurface rock, which flowed onto the surface through cracks and vents. These basalt flows formed the *maria*.

Today the Moon is almost inactive in geologic terms. Its internal

Where Did the Moon Come From?

For hundreds of years scientists pondered the origin of the Moon. Did it solidify out of the Solar System's original cloud of matter, like Earth? Was it a wandering body captured by Earth's gravity? In the 1980s scientists developed a new theory. Most now agree that the Moon was created by a giant impact that took place not long after Earth formed.

Around 4.5 billion years ago, Earth collided with or was struck by a smaller planet, perhaps the size of Mars. The smaller planet was shattered. Its heavy core sank into Earth, merging with Earth's core. Its lighter materials were thrown out into space, along with additional material from Earth's mantle. The rocky debris and dust formed a cloud that orbited Earth. The Moon was born when chunks of this cloud collided, stuck together, and swept up still more debris. Astronauts have collected samples of Moon rock 4.3 billion years old, dating from soon after the Moon's birth.

According to the impact theory of the Moon's formation, a smaller planet struck the young Earth. This smaller planet's core disappeared into Earth's core, but material from both worlds escaped into space, where it collected and solidified into the Moon.

heat has died, and there is no evidence of active volcanoes. Instruments left on the lunar surface by the *Apollo* astronauts operated for six years, gathering data and sending it to Earth. They recorded occasional small moonquakes, but unlike earthquakes, these are not caused by plate tectonics. Moonquakes result from impacts, the lunar crust settling under the weight of the basalt *maria*, or minor variations in Earth's gravitational pull at different points in the Moon's orbit. The Moon does not have a magnetic field like Earth's, but some of its rocks are magnetic, which means that in the past, when it was more geologically active, it probably produced a magnetic field.

Scientists know that the Moon has an outer crust and an inner mantle. The crust is 44 miles (70 kilometers) thick on average, but it is thicker on the far side of the Moon and thinner under the *maria*, for unknown reasons. Large amounts of aluminum, calcium, and silicon are present in parts of the crust. The thick, solid mantle makes up most of the Moon's mass. It contains heavier materials than the crust, including the basalt that once flowed out across the *maria*. Some researchers believe that a dense core rich in metals such as iron lies beneath the mantle. If so, the core probably measures less than 560

Lunar Facts and Figures

Distance from Earth: 239,000 miles (384,400 kilometers)
Diameter at Equator: 2,160 miles (3,476 kilometers)
Period of Revolution around Earth: 27.3 days
Speed of Revolution: 22,870 miles (36,800 kilometers) per hour
Period of Rotation on Axis: 29.5 days
Gravity: One-sixth of Earth's
High and Low Temperatures: 214 degrees F (101 degrees C); -300 degrees F (-184 degrees C)

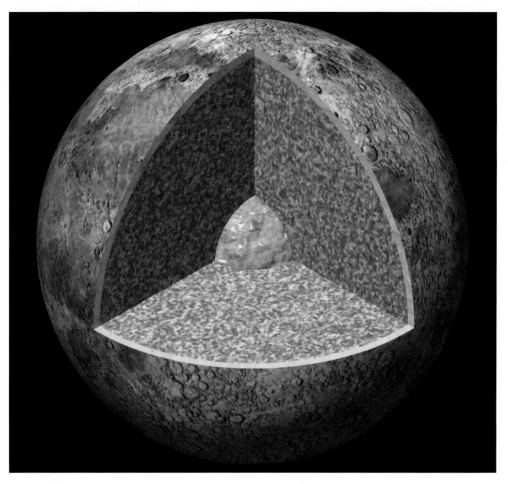

Most of the Moon's mass consists of its mantle, the thick layer beneath the outer crust. The Moon may have a small, dense core, as shown in this graphic, but scientists do not yet know whether such a core exists much less its makeup.

miles (900 kilometers) across and contains less than 4 percent of the Moon's mass. Lunar geologists are eager for a better understanding of the mantle and an answer to the question of a core. They may not be able to solve these problems, however, without more exploration on and beneath the powdery, cratered surface of the Moon.

5

FUTURE EXPLORATION

Earth is the only planet that human beings can easily explore, and much remains to be learned about our world. Earth-science research does more than satisfy the curiosity of white-coated scientists in laboratories—it may protect individuals, communities, and the entire planet. And although no one has visited the Moon since the Apollo program ended in 1972, the exploration of our satellite is far from over. Some astronomers and lunar scientists hope that we are entering a new era of interest in the Moon.

TERRESTRIAL MYSTERIES

The twentieth century brought breakthroughs in the understanding of plate tectonics, including the forces that cause earthquakes and volcanic eruptions. In the coming years, scientists hope to learn more about quakes and eruptions so that they can predict when and where these events will occur. Science cannot prevent natural earth movements, but accurate, dependable warnings would save lives by giving people time to get out of the way.

Improved weather forecasting could also save lives and property. Meteorologists hope that as they learn more about the planet's climate and weather systems, they will be better able to predict events

Made from photos taken by an orbiting research satellite, this image shows the shadow of the Moon moving across Earth's surface during a 1991 solar eclipse. The shadow travels from the Pacific coast of South America (bottom right) through

One lively area of research concerns the impacts of asteroids or comets into Earth. Many scientists think that such impacts caused mass extinctions in the past, including the disappearance of the dinosaurs.

such as tornadoes, hurricanes, and the giant waves called tsunamis. Climatology—the study of Earth's climates—is the focus of many research projects currently underway or planned for the future. Climatologists want to know more about how air and water currents govern climate and weather around the world. Using clues from the past such as fossilized plants and ancient ice from Greenland and Antarctica, they are also finding out more about how Earth's climate and weather have changed over long periods of time. Dramatic climate changes such as ice ages and warming trends are part of Earth's history. By learning about the causes of such changes, scientists hope to be able to predict future climate developments.

Many climatological studies focus on the question: How much are human activities contributing to climate change? Global warming is a major concern. We now know that Earth is growing warmer, and it is probably going to keep getting warmer. In 2000 the U.S. Global Change Research Program predicted that average U.S. temperatures will rise from 5 to 10 degrees Fahrenheit during the twenty-first century. The increase may produce hotter summers, more severe rain and flooding in some places, and more drastic water shortages in others. Worldwide climate change in modern times has already had an effect. According to the U.S. National Climatic Data Center, higher temperatures and melting icecaps have caused the oceans to rise about 4 inches (10 centimeters) in the past 100 years. The rise over the next 100 years could be as much as 24 inches (60 centimeters), enough to drown some islands and flood low-lying coastal areas worldwide. But although scientists know that global warming is occurring, they do not yet know how much of it is caused by human activities, such as burning fossil fuels and cutting forests. Some experts believe that humans can stop—or at least slow—global warming by changing their activities. Others argue that global warming is part of a little-understood cycle of climate variations and would continue no matter what humans did. Only further research will settle the question.

Astronomers and geologists would like to know more about how the Solar System formed and what the young Earth was like. To answer their questions, they may have to turn to the Moon, where rock from early in the Solar System's history is preserved on the surface. Scientists also believe that particles from the Sun, trapped in the Moon's regolith, may hold clues to the history of the Sun over billions of years.

BACK TO THE MOON?

Exploration of the Moon did not end when *Apollo 17* returned to Earth in 1972. The Soviet Union sent three successful probes to the Moon between 1973 and 1976. In 1990 Japan launched a probe that orbited the Moon, and four years later the American *Clementine* probe carried out a photographic and mapping survey of the Moon.

The most ambitious Moon mission of recent years was NASA's *Lunar Prospector*, launched in 1998. This unmanned probe orbited the Moon for eighteen months, mapping the Moon's gravity pattern and the small, local magnetic fields given off by deposits of magnetized rock. One of the most important tasks of the *Lunar Prospector* was to search for evidence of ice in permanently shadowed craters at the Moon's north and south poles. Some of the photographs and chemical analyses that the probe sent back to Earth suggest that water ice may exist in these locations. If it does exist, it is the only known water on the Moon. In 1999 NASA deliberately crashed the *Lunar Prospector* into a crater at the south pole. This allowed scientists to analyze the dust thrown skyward by the impact for signs of water vapor. Although this experiment did not produce concrete proof that the Moon has water ice, many scientists believe that the ice is there.

Why is ice on the Moon so important? If it does exist, future lunar explorers and scientists—maybe even colonists—could use it as a source of water and perhaps also of oxygen, which water contains (lunar surface rocks also contain considerable oxygen). Exploration, research, and settlement on the Moon would be much cheaper and easier if people did not have to bring all the necessary water and oxygen from Earth. When active exploration of the Moon's surface resumes, one of the explorers' first tasks will be to search for ice.

At the dawn of the twenty-first century, no governmental space agency has announced plans to send humans to the Moon. The European Space Agency is planning an orbital probe, and NASA will likely send another probe at some point as well. Some space scientists

An artist's impression of the Lunar Prospector *nearing the Moon.*

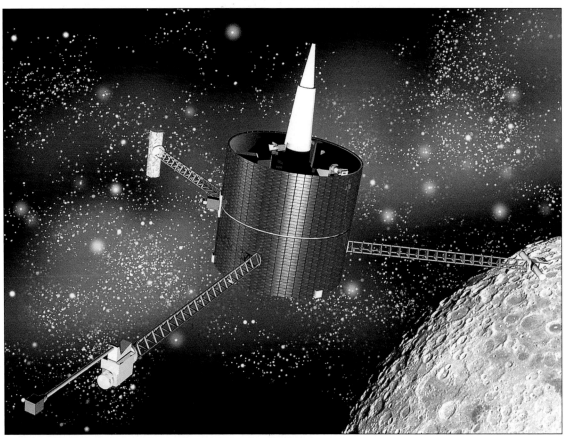

think that the next manned mission to the Moon may be funded by corporations or private investors rather than by a government.

One way or another, human beings are probably going to return to our one natural satellite. The Moon is the perfect place for an astronomical observatory—a large telescope would be easier to build and maintain on the Moon than in orbit, and the airless Moon would offer better visibility than Earth. A lunar base could also serve as the launch point for missions farther into the Solar System. Perhaps someday a base will be built using the Moon's own resources. Regolith, which has insulating properties, might make an excellent building material.

Moon bases now exist only in science fiction and in predictions for the future. Yet we have the technology to create an outpost on the Moon, and someone, someday, will almost certainly do so.

A way might be found to release the oxygen locked up in the surface rocks, and the solar power of the Moon's two-week-long daylight periods could meet at least part of a base's energy needs. The Moon might even have mineral resources that could be mined and shipped to Earth. Someday, perhaps, children raised on the Moon will be as fascinated by the blue Earth hanging in their sky as we Earth-dwellers have always been by the Moon.

Earth Facts and Figures

Rank in Solar System: third planet from the Sun, fifth largest in size
Distance from Sun: 93 million miles (150 million kilometers)
Period of Revolution around Sun: 365.25 days (one year)
Period of Rotation on Axis: 23 hours, 56 minutes, 4 seconds (one day)
Distance around Equator: 25,000 miles (40,000 kilometers)
Diameter from Pole to Pole: 7,900 miles (12,700 kilometers)
Total Surface Area: 197 million square miles (510 million square kilometers)
Surface Covered by Water: 71 percent

Glossary

asteroid rock-metal body orbiting the Sun between Mars and Jupiter

astronomer one who studies space and the objects in it

atmosphere layer of gases surrounding a world; air

celestial having to do with the sky, the heavens, or astronomy

crater pit, hole, or flat area, usually with a ring of hills around it, created by an explosion or impact

evolve change of develop over time; in biology, related to evolution, the process by which living beings pass on naturally occurring changes, or mutations, to their offspring, eventually forming new species

gravity force that holds matter together and draws objects toward one another

hemisphere half of a globe, either the northern, southern, eastern, or western portion

interstellar between the stars

lunar having to do with the Moon

meteorite body of rock or metal from space that crashes onto a planet

meteorologist scientist who studies the weather

micrometeorite very small meteorite

microorganism organism so small that it can be seen only through a microscope

orbit to revolve around another object; path followed by an object as it revolves around another object

organic having to do with life; related to or produced by living organisms

organism living thing

probe machine or tool sent to gather information and report it to the sender

satellite object that revolves in orbit around a planet; natural satellites are called moons

sensor instrument that can detect and record information, such as light waves, sounds, X-rays, or gravitational and magnetic readings

solar having to do with the Sun

Solar System all bodies that revolve around or are influenced by the Sun, including planets, moons, asteroids, and comets

telescope device that uses magnifying lenses, sometimes together with mirrors, to enlarge the image of something viewed through it

FIND OUT MORE

BOOKS FOR YOUNG READERS

Asimov, Isaac. *The Earth's Moon*. Milwaukee: Gareth Stevens, 1988.

Bourgeois, Paulette. *The Moon*. Buffalo, NY: Kids Can Press, 1997.

Branley, Franklyn M. *The Moon Seems to Change*. New York: Harper & Row, 1987.

———. *What the Moon Is Like*. New York: HarperCollins, 2000.

Couper, Heather. *The Moon*. New York: Franklin Watts, 1986.

Fradin, Dennis. *Earth*. Chicago: Childrens Press, 1989.

Gibbons, Gail. *Planet Earth, Inside Out*. New York: Morrow Junior Books, 1995.

———. *The Moon Book*. New York: Holiday House, 1997.

Graham, Ian. *The Best Book of the Moon*. New York: Kingfisher, 1999.

Kerrod, Robin. *Planet Earth*. Minneapolis: Lerner, 2000.

———. *The Moon*. Minneapolis: Lerner, 2000.

Lauber, Patricia. *Seeing Earth from Space*. New York: Orchard Books, 1990.

———. *You're Aboard Spaceship Earth*. New York: HarperCollins, 1996.

Llewellyn, Claire. *Our Planet Earth*. New York: Scholastic, 1997.

Moore, Patrick. *The Sun and Moon*. Brookfield, CT: Copper Beech Books, 1995.

Nicolson, Cynthia P. *The Earth*. Buffalo, NY: Kids Can Press, 1997.

Planet Earth. Alexandria, VA: Time-Life, 1992.

Ride, Sally, and Tom O'Shaughnessy. *The Third Planet: Exploring the Earth from Space*. New York: Crown, 1994.

Simon, Seymour. *Our Planet in Space*. New York: Four Winds Press, 1984.

————. *The Moon*. New York: Four Winds Press, 1984.

Taylor, Barbara. *Earth Explained: A Beginner's Guide to Our Planet*. New York: Henry Holt, 1997.

Vogt, Gregory. *Earth*. Brookfield, CT: Millbrook, 1996.

WEBSITES

The following Internet sites offer information about and pictures of Earth and the Moon, along with links to other sites:

www.bbc.co.uk/planets/index.html Home page of the British Broadcasting Corporation's Planets site, companion to a television series. The site has sections devoted to Earth and the Moon.

www.pds.jpl.nasa.gov/planets/welcome/html Home page of the Welcome to the Planets site, maintained for NASA by the California Institute of Technology. The site contains images from NASA's planetary exploration program, including many images of Earth and the Moon.

www.seds.org/billa/tnp.html Home page of The Nine Planets, a multimedia tour of the Solar System. Its section on Luna, the Moon, has information on everything from mythology to lunar exploration.

www.nationalgeographic.com/solarsystem.splash.html Entry to the National Geographic Society's virtual Solar System, with a variety of images, including three-dimensional fly-bys of Earth and the Moon.

www.fourmilab.ch/earthview/vplanet.html The Earth and Moon Viewer site has many maps and images of our planet and its satellite.

Interactive features let you view them from vantage points you choose.

www.solarviews.com/homepage.htm Astronomer Calvin J. Hamilton developed this Views of the Universe site, which is maintained by the Hawaiian Astronomical Society. It offers both images and information about Earth and the Moon.

www.kidsastronomy.com A website designed especially for young people features material on Earth and the Moon in its section on the Solar System.

www.nasm.edu/ceps/etp The National Air and Space Museum's Center for Earth and Planetary Studies developed this site, called Exploring the Planets. It has a section on Earth and one on the Moon.

www.windows.ucar.edu Funded by NASA and developed by a team of scientists, artists, and educators, the Windows on the Universe site is rich in graphics and is devoted to earth and space sciences.

www.usgs.gov/ The home page of the United States Geological Survey is an entry portal to an enormous amount of information about earth sciences, including an easy-to-read handbook on plate tectonics, accounts of seafloor mapping projects, and overviews of current and future research.

ABOUT THE AUTHOR

Rebecca Stefoff, author of many books on scientific subjects for young readers, has been fascinated with space ever since she spent summer nights lying on her lawn in Indiana and gazing up at the Milky Way. Her first telescope was a gift from parents, who encouraged her interest in other worlds and in this one. Today she lives in Portland, Oregon, close to the clear skies and superb stargazing of eastern Oregon's deserts.

INDEX

Page numbers for illustrations are in boldface.